IDEAS IN PSYCHOANALYSIS

The Superego

Priscill

Series editor: Ivan Ward

ICON BOOKS UK

TOTEM BOOKS USA

Published in the UK in 2001
by Icon Books Ltd., Grange Road,
Duxford, Cambridge CB2 4QF
E-mail: info@iconbooks.co.uk
www.iconbooks.co.uk

Published in the USA in 2001
by Totem Books
Inquiries to: Icon Books Ltd.,
Grange Road, Duxford
Cambridge CB2 4QF, UK

Sold in the UK, Europe, South Africa
and Asia by Faber and Faber Ltd.,
3 Queen Square, London WC1N 3AU
or their agents

Distributed to the trade in the USA
by National Book Network Inc.,
4720 Boston Way, Lanham,
Maryland 20706

Distributed in the UK, Europe,
South Africa and Asia by
Macmillan Distribution Ltd.,
Houndmills, Basingstoke RG21 6XS

Distributed in Canada by
Penguin Books Canada,
10 Alcorn Avenue, Suite 300,
Toronto, Ontario M4V 3B2

Published in Australia in 2001
by Allen & Unwin Pty. Ltd.,
PO Box 8500, 83 Alexander Street,
Crows Nest, NSW 2065

ISBN 1 84046 246 9

Series editor: Ivan Ward

Typesetting by Hands Fotoset

Printed and bound in the UK by
Cox & Wyman Ltd., Reading

Introduction

Everyone has a superego. Not everyone calls it a superego. Some people call it a conscience, or even a guilty conscience; some people call it morality. But whatever it's called, everyone has one. Your superego is most recognisable as (but, as we will see, is not limited to) that voice inside your head which won't let you do something wrong (illegal, immoral, unkind) even when nobody else would know. And which punishes you from inside when you succumb to temptation and do something that you know you shouldn't have done . . . and sometimes even when you haven't.

You could think about it as being your 'conscience', but the Freudian idea of a superego is not exactly the same as a conscience, although they share many similar qualities and characteristics. One of the biggest differences between the very ancient idea of 'conscience' and the psychoanalytic extension of it called 'the superego', is that the concept of the superego recognises that there is often very little relation between what a person consciously thinks is permissible, and what the superego actually allows him or her to do. Or, to put it the other way round: we can sometimes feel very guilty, or experience a vague feeling of badness, without having much awareness of what we've done to make us feel guilty and bad. People often, for instance, find themselves feeling anxious when questioned at customs at the airport, or pulled over by a policeman for a routine check, even when they can't think of anything they've done that is actually illegal.

To further complicate matters, sometimes our superego speaks quite directly and straightforwardly inside us: 'Get down to work NOW; you've been procrastinating long enough!', or 'DO NOT eat another chocolate!', or 'If you leave the dirty dishes on the table, you'll just have to do them when you come home, so do them before you go out!' Sometimes it is more punitive: 'You are a nasty, unkind person to treat your sister like that; you REALLY are a nasty unkind person to treat your sister like that.' And sometimes it is very punitive: 'You are an unspeakably, horribly nasty person. You don't deserve anybody's friendship or love. You only deserve to be miserable.' All of these are ways the superego can directly instruct or attack us from inside ourselves.

On the other hand, often it is too painful to have such a voice inside, so we somehow manage to perceive it as being located in other people: 'My sister hates me for being a little tiny bit unkind to her – she is oversensitive and really cold and always makes me feel bad.' 'My boss is forever accusing me of being late.' 'I know those people think I'm fat and disgusting when they see me eating chocolate.' And frequently our superego directs us, or prohibits us from doing things, and we're not even aware of the process; we're perhaps just aware that something inexplicable is going on inside us: 'I don't know why, but I just don't feel like going to that party.'; 'I don't know . . . I can just never relax until I've finished all my homework.'; 'I'm completely happy being a little fish in a little pond; no great ambitions for me!' At these times, our superego is invisible, or inaudible, or – as psychoanalysts would describe it – *unconscious*. We don't know that it is affecting us, but in fact it is having a powerful effect on our feelings, our wishes and our behaviour.

In this essay, I explain what psychoanalysts mean by 'the superego' and why it is a useful and important concept. In order to show where it fits into psychoanalytic theory, first I discuss Freud's two models of how the mind works. Then I address the question: 'Is the superego necessary?' (Why do we have to have a superego? Wouldn't we be better off without one?) I fill in the descriptions outlined briefly below: what a person's superego sounds and feels like; what it is like when it is inside us telling us what to do and what not to do, and how it can be projected outside, so that we feel other people are criticising and judging us; or even how we can turn it on others, so that it judges other people to protect ourselves from its harshness. And I ask: 'What are the signs of a superego working unconsciously?'

I end with a discussion on the origins of the superego – the events of childhood that leave each of us with an internal critical and judgemental agency – and explore some of the different views psychoanalysts currently hold about these origins.

The place of the superego in psychoanalytic theory

The superego is one part of Freud's second and final theory of how the mind works. Freud's first theory was called the 'topographical model', and it divided the mind into two areas: a Conscious/Pre-conscious area that contains all the thoughts and feelings of which we are already aware or could easily become aware; and, metaphorically beneath it, a much larger Unconscious, full of drives and impulses of which we cannot be directly aware. These drives and impulses were thought to be inborn and instinctive and to seek immediate satisfaction – food or drink or sexual satisfaction. They also often come into conflict with other, socially approved, learned behaviour, and therein lies the friction between these two areas of the mind: the Unconscious pressing for satisfaction of its impulses, and a conscious, rational, socialised part of the mind that contains a critical agency that forbids the satisfaction of these wishes. We cannot observe unconscious wishes directly, but we can observe how they push past the critical agency and manifest themselves indirectly in our behaviour: our 'mistakes', our jokes, our dreams and, more troublingly, our neurotic symptoms.

The topographical model, in which conflict exists between Consciousness (which includes those thoughts and wishes that are not currently conscious, but that could become conscious the moment our attention is turned to them – Freud called this area the 'Pre-conscious') and the Unconscious, was very useful in directing attention to and stimulating the exploration of this vast area of our minds that profoundly influences our behaviour and thoughts, but of which we are usually unaware.

The problems with the topographical model were twofold: in the first place, it assumed that the critical agency – that part of our mind that decides what we are allowed to be conscious of – is also a part of the conscious mind. That is, it was assumed to be rational, and opposed to instinctive wishes and demands. But Freud and his followers soon began to realise that their patients often seemed to have an *unconscious* critical agency – they didn't know they were being criticised or punished from the inside, yet they suffered in ways that indicated they were. Indeed, Freud thought that patients often came to him with an unconscious need for punishment. For example, a number of patients seemed to feel profoundly uncomfortable as they began to recover from their painful symptoms, as though they felt guilty about being well and, in an odd way, had felt better when they were suffering.

Second, the topographical model assumed that a person's defences against the emergence of unconscious wishes were themselves conscious; by definition, that which was opposed to unconscious impulses was part of the Conscious/Pre-conscious system. But again it began to be clear that many defences against unconscious impulses are themselves unconscious, and that the area of the mind that could be described as unconscious contains more than simply biological impulses and infantile wishes. It was largely in order to deal with these problems with the theory that Freud gradually developed his second and final model of the mind, the 'structural theory', which continues to take account of the consciousness/unconsciousness divide, but is not limited to it.[1]

The structural model of the mind pictures the mind as consisting of three parts: the *id*, the *ego* and the *superego*. In the id, Freud located all the instincts and drives we are born with: our sexual and aggressive impulses, as well as our inborn drives to seek food, water and warmth and so on. These biological needs are largely unconscious and do not take account of reality. They are often in conflict with the demands society makes upon us: if we were all 'id' we would have trouble getting along in our world. The second part of our mind, the ego, develops out of the id over the first days and weeks and months after birth, as the infant slowly begins to perceive the external world and to adapt himself to it: to learn how to get his mother's attention, for example, or to remember that the sight of her usually means he will be comforted. This increasingly rational, organising, tuned-into-the-world part of the mind, the ego, contains the capacity for rational thought, for planning and remembering. But interfering, often, with the ego's functioning, is the superego. The superego is the third part of this three-part system. It grows out of the ego as the young child incorporates the rules of its parents and society, as we shall see, and it becomes a powerful force of its own in the mind of the individual. Its power comes from its capacity to create guilt and the bad feelings connected with guilt, and it can dictate our behaviour and even our thoughts. While the superego can help the individual to conform to the basic rules and laws of the society he lives in, it can also sometimes become the most powerful and even the most destructive part of his personality.

What good is a superego if it only makes you feel bad?

We could start addressing this point by asking a few other questions. What makes civilised behaviour possible? Why do most people conform to the law? Why do some people break the law? And why do most of us not break the law even when it would seem to be to our advantage to do so and we can be certain we wouldn't get caught?

In trying to address these questions, most people would look for the answers in the notion of a conscience, as I have already said – we would have a bad conscience if we broke the law, for instance. What Freud understood was that conscience is not just about a kind of rational moral code; conscience, he said, is deeply related to a sense of guilt. Our respect for social relations, and law and order, is not simply imposed on us by the society we live in, but comes from a need that begins in infancy and early childhood: a need to obey, honour and maintain the social order in which we live. The fact that many people fall outside this description – criminals, for instance, and, in a very different way, revolutionaries who want to change the social order – does not make this basic premise untrue. On the contrary, it suggests what psychoanalysis has shown time and time again: that our wish for order develops in relation to, and in a permanent struggle with, other more destructive and also more creative wishes. Conflict is in our very nature: conflict between the wish to preserve and maintain and the wish to destroy and tear apart; conflict between the wish to stay the same and the wish to change and grow; conflict between our most precious loving impulses, and our powerfully destructive ones. The mental structure that controls and moderates these conflicts is what psychoanalysts call the superego.

The recognition that conscience is deeply related to a sense of guilt was an important one. Guilt, here, does not mean guilt in the eyes of the law, as in 'He was guilty of the crime'. What we are talking about is a personal sense of guilt, of *feeling* guilty. And of course, as we all know, this is not the same as being guilty in anyone else's eyes. Someone can be guilty of a crime and not feel guilty. Or someone can feel guilty while not in fact being guilty of anything. Such a person might not have the faintest idea why he feels so guilty, since his reasons for feeling guilty might be out of reach of the conscious mind. Feeling guilty is, at the least, a very unpleasant feeling. Sometimes it is worse, when from within there is a voice ceaselessly criticising and castigating us until it invades our thoughts, and our life feels entirely taken over by a sense of guilt. At these times we are forced to do something to assuage or get rid of such painful feelings: we have to try to make things better, to repair the damage, or we begin to blame someone else. At its worst, when guilt is at its most extreme and remorseless, it is literally intolerable. It can lead a person to seek terrible punishment for himself or it can turn with extraordinary ferocity on others who are held to blame. At its very worst, it can lead to suicide.

Perhaps now we can begin to answer the questions asked at the beginning of this section: by and large people behave in a civilised way, do not break the law, do maintain the social order, because they would feel guilty if they were to behave differently.

Freud argued that civilisation – by which he meant social and cultural organisation – developed, and could be maintained, because human beings go through experiences in their infancy and childhood that establish inside each individual a propensity to feel guilty when they have broken the rules – a critical agency which he called the superego. I discuss how this happens later on in this essay. For the moment, though, it is important to know that at a very early period in their lives, small children take inside themselves, and identify with, their parents' prohibitions. Their superego is like the voice of their parents inside themselves, sometimes praising them for 'good' behaviour, but more often scolding or even punishing them severely for what the superego feels is bad behaviour. This voice of authority that once belonged to the parents becomes part of the self, confronting the rest of the self ('the ego') and making demands upon it.

In Freud's view, the establishment of this internal critical agency in the development of each individual makes civilisation possible. Our ability to live together in complex social units – villages, cities, nations – requires that as individuals we repress many of our powerful instinctual urges; we have to deprive ourselves of immediate sexual gratification, and untrammelled aggressiveness, because not to do so would threaten the social structure we live in. The rewards of civilised life are many; above all, life is more secure in a civilised society. But such security is exchanged for severe restrictions placed on innate human tendencies. We are left with a seemingly more moral enterprise than in certain, more primitive forms of social order. But the aggressiveness that has been repressed by civilisation is channelled back towards the self in the form of a harsh moral conscience, which we experience as guilt. Guilt, then, is part of human nature and part of the human experience. This is the process that Freud attributed to the mental structure that he named the superego. It is the necessary guardian of morality; it keeps the order. It is also the price we pay for civilisation. A strong superego, says Freud,

is the most important problem in the development of civilisation [. . . since] *the price we pay for our advance in civilisation is a loss of happiness through the heightening of this sense of guilt.*[2]

It is important to notice that the social order Freud outlines, and the morality underlying it, is based on fear. Although Freud often stressed the fact that parents are not only feared but deeply loved,[3] the moral conscience deriving from the superego he describes is fear- rather than love-based. As one feared one's father's stern reproach as a child, so one fears the stern reproach of one's superego as an adult.

However, most people would feel that while we are often 'good' because we are afraid not to be – afraid of feeling guilty – we are also often 'good' because we have, and make use of, more loving, generous, caring impulses. As well as aggressive drives, people also often seem to have a tendency to be decent. And this tendency is derived from the same processes that establish the more punitive superego inside: an internalisation of parental qualities at a very early age. The way in which these internalisations and identifications take place, how they interact with each other and with the child's own unconscious impulses and phantasies about his parents, has been explored in great depth by analysts after Freud; in particular by Melanie Klein.[4]

Where to find your superego

Inside and perfectly conscious

Inside your own mind is the most obvious place to look for your superego and to begin to study how it works. Most people will quickly be able to think of their own superego voice as it is experienced in their thoughts: 'If you don't get up and offer your seat to that woman, you are going to feel really bad.' 'You could just pocket that £5 note you found on the floor of the shop, but you'll feel bad if you do.' 'Okay, you got away with pocketing the £5; you really should be ashamed of yourself. What kind of a creep are you?' 'You've just said something extremely nasty to that woman; how could you do such a thing?' These are ordinary temptations and failures and most of us get punished by ourselves in an ordinary way for them. And most of us recognise that a feeling of guilt is just that: the way we punish ourselves for doing things we feel we shouldn't. At this level our superegos function in a logical and therefore easily understandable way: we know what we've done wrong, and we know that we feel guilty and why.

But some people suffer much more profoundly, and seemingly illogically, from their 'guilty conscience'. These people feel so bad, so guilty at the possibility of doing, or even *thinking*, something that they feel they shouldn't, that either their behaviour is seriously constricted, or they suffer pervasive and extremely debilitating guilt.

A little girl in therapy explained that she knew it was wicked to think about what was underneath Christ's loincloth when she was in church; she tried desperately to stop herself from thinking about it, but to no avail. She was tortured by guilty feelings and felt that she deserved to be punished. One way of describing what was going on inside her mind would be to say she had a harsh and cruel superego that punished her not only for what she did, but also for what she thought. From the point of view of this internal authority, thoughts are as condemnable as actions. And, of course, therapy for this little girl meant understanding something about this super-ego: where she got it from and why it was so punishing.

A well-known politician told a story recently that when he was a little boy he used to have to ask permission from his teacher to be 'rowdy'. 'Is it time to be rowdy now, Sir?', he remembers asking. This is a picture of a child afraid to be an ordinary child; afraid that his superego would punish him severely if he 'let himself go'. He, too, had a harsh superego.

Seeing or hearing about children who punish themselves mentally is particularly painful, and makes us wonder where this cruel voice comes from. We might think such children have been repeatedly told they are bad by particularly strict parents. This is often not at all the case, and in fact the severity of a child's superego seems in no way to correspond to the severity of the treatment a particular individual has actually received. It is as if the superego is only like the strictest aspects of the child's parents, and totally ignores the parents' love and concern. (Every parent will recognise the situation where their children seem only to remember the time the parents became really angry, or the time they were yelled at, or the time they were not allowed to watch the television even though they hadn't done anything wrong!) Psychoanalysts understand this discrepancy between the harshness of a person's superego and the actual treatment they received as a child as an important illustration of the process by which the superego is established: the child internalises his parents who are viewed through the child's own unconscious aggression towards them. So the superego is characterised by a double aggression: the aggressive, authoritative aspects of the parents, augmented by the child's unconscious aggression.

Inside yourself but not really conscious

Interestingly, by far the biggest part of our superego is unconscious. What that means is that we are motivated by feelings – of which we are unaware – about the things we do and the things we think, and sometimes about things that we're not even aware that we think! This sounds strange and maybe impossible, but psychoanalysts find evidence all the time that people are feeling guilty without knowing they are about things they weren't aware of doing or thinking.

An example: a woman decided to consult a psychoanalyst about something that had begun to worry her. This woman was married to a man she loved deeply, but she was unable to enjoy having sexual intercourse with him. There was, as far as she could tell, no reason why she shouldn't enjoy it. Still, she found that she didn't enjoy it; in fact, she found that she felt mildly depressed afterwards. Consciously she felt she had done nothing wrong, and consciously she did not feel guilty. And yet she was aware that all was not as it should be, and that her capacity for enjoyment was painfully inhibited. She hoped that psychoanalysis would be able to help her with this problem. In analysis she began gradually to get a picture of some of the forces that were playing a part in the situation. As a very small girl, she had loved her mother deeply, but when her little sister was born, she turned against her mother and became a 'daddy's girl'. She remembers having been pretty horrid to her mother for several years, but she eventually outgrew this stage and had developed a reasonable relationship with her mother. Her father died when she was a teenager, and her mother never remarried, remaining a widow for the rest of her life. In analysis the patient gradually became aware of her very mixed and turbulent feelings about her parents: her love for her mother and then her resentment, envy and jealousy of her; her little-girl wish to be better than her mother, to please her father more than her mother did; her hatred of her mother for not, somehow, being able to keep her father alive; her admiration for her mother's courage, mixed with a kind of triumph about growing into a sexual woman herself when her mother was without

a sexual partner; her terrible, though unconscious, guilt, based on her very real love for
her mother, about having, as she put it,
'reversed the roles – now I'm the only one with
a husband!'. This unconscious guilt at her
unconscious feelings of triumph over her
mother prevented her from being able to be
fully sexual with her husband until both the
triumph and the guilt were uncovered and
understood in analysis.

As in this case, depressed feelings, mild or
more severe, are often a sign of unconscious
guilt. Depression can itself take many forms:
lethargy, tiredness, sleeplessness, a vague sense
of unhappiness, or lack of pleasure or enthusiasm. In other words, while your superego
can attack you by making you feel guilty, it can
also attack in much more surreptitious ways,
making you feel depressed, or just 'under par'.
It can sap the pleasure from your life and leave
you feeling that life is meaningless. While you

don't consciously *feel* guilty, you are being punished for something you unconsciously feel guilty about.

What sort of thing might we feel unconsciously guilty about? Here is a vignette from another patient in analysis. This young woman came to analysis because she was finding it difficult to have meaningful relationships or to enjoy her work which she felt was potentially exciting and interesting, but which she had found herself approaching with less and less enthusiasm. Her history included a terrible tragedy in the family: her younger sister had been injured in a swimming accident when the two girls were on holiday as teenagers. The sister was now extremely and permanently disabled. The patient was aware of feeling sad and sorry, and sometimes burdened, by the sister's disablement – for which she was in no way responsible. But she was not aware of how guilty she felt about it until she had a dream that reminded her of an event that had taken place when she was very young – about three years old. She remembered being at the supper table with her father and big brother while the little sister, at that time a small baby, was being fed and put to bed by her mother. And she remembered the terrible feeling that there wasn't enough food for her and that she hated the baby. She began to cry and complain and have a temper tantrum, and eventually she was sent from the table.

As she described the situation as she remembered it, there was in fact plenty of food on the table. It became clear that what she was missing was her mother, and the thought of the baby being fed at her mother's breast filled her with painful feelings of deprivation and jealousy and also hatred of this baby who was having everything she herself wanted.

The sister's actual tragic accident felt like a fulfilment of the patient's very ordinary hostile wishes towards her. The patient couldn't put together her memory of her hostility towards her baby sister when she was a child, and her sadness at her disablement, because to do so would have led to intolerable guilt.

Instead, the connections were not made and the guilt remained unconscious and the patient punished herself for her infantile aggression by denying herself any joy or satisfaction in her own life.

An episode in the life of Charles Dickens, the famous 19th-century novelist, if looked at through this lens, could perhaps provide us with a picture of unacknowledged guilt. In 1858, Dickens left his wife, Catherine, suddenly and cruelly after 30 years of marriage. His friends and family were shocked and puzzled at what seemed inexplicably cold and abrupt behaviour: at first he literally built a wall in the marital bedroom to separate his area from hers and then, when that didn't sufficiently remove her from his presence, he insisted that she leave the house. With implacable hatred, he tried to alienate her children from her; Dickens himself stayed on in the family home with all but the smallest child, and with his wife's sister, Georgina, to look after him. In the immediate aftermath of the separation, Dickens was hateful about Catherine and 'remorselessly vindictive' towards anyone he felt to be 'siding' with her. He was full of self-righteousness and self-justification. Dickens was convinced that he was absolutely in the right and insisted his bewildered friends agree with him.

For a while, the author seemed to be relieved at the changes he had made in his life. But gradually his behaviour became a source of real worry to his friends and doctors. He began a 'whirlwind' of activity, including long tours around the British Isles in which he would perform in theatres, acting out readings from his works. The choice of readings changed over the weeks, except that one piece was invariably retained: Dickens insisted on including the 'Death of Nancy', from his novel *Oliver Twist*, over and over again. In this scene, Bill Sikes, a hateful criminal, viciously murders his gentle, good and innocent common-law wife, Nancy. Dickens performed both parts – that of the innocent woman, brutally attacked, and that of her ferocious assailant. As weeks and months went by, the performances took on an increasingly frantic quality. Dickens reported to friends that he was finding it difficult to distinguish between himself and his text, and after each rehearsal, as he walked the streets he had 'the vague sensation of being "wanted"':

Through the fall and winter [. . .] In England, Scotland and Ireland, he went on 'murdering

Nancy' with a regularity that became addictive.[5]

He became extremely ill, friends reported him looking

desperately aged and worn; with lines in his cheeks and round the eyes now in deep furrows; there [was] a weariness in his gaze and a general air of fatigue and depression about him.[6]

Dickens' recent biographer, Fred Kaplan, writes:

When [Dickens] enacted Sikes' killing of Nancy, he created the stage illusion that he was Sikes, that his will and his heart were committed to the crime. They were. In repeatedly murdering her, he expressed himself with displaced violence against the horrible women of his life, his mother and his wife. [. . .] In murdering Nancy, he committed a crime of vengeance [. . .] available to him only within fiction. So powerful was his identification with Sikes that not even Sikes' death could free him from the emotional grip of that identification.[7]

And after the performances, Kaplan continues:

An unworthy criminal still prowled on the loose, within himself. After the reading, when he left the theatre, he almost expected to be arrested in the streets. He looked over his shoulder to see who was pursuing him.[8]

When reading this distressing and disturbing account, it is hard to avoid the conclusion that there was more going into the enactment of this fictional scene than was contained in the story of Bill Sikes and Nancy. One is almost forced to consider that there was another murder being played out on the stage each night; that, unable to confront his guilt and shame at his treatment of his wife, Dickens compulsively had to enact and re-enact it. I would suggest, then, that what was pursuing Dickens as he left the theatre each night was his own superego.

The very harsh superego inside

One of the most important areas to look at when exploring how the superego works is the relative gentleness or harshness of any particular person's superego. A healthy person has a superego that, by and large, helps him to feel good about himself and punishes him by making him feel guilty only when he behaves badly. A healthy superego is like a kind but firm parent: it has rules, but it is also forgiving of transgressions. It can be reasoned with and mitigated: if I behave badly, recognise that I have behaved badly, and try to make reparation, my superego usually gives me some credit for it and forgives me. Reparation – trying to make good the damage you've done – is related to the religious and spiritual notion of redemption; it always implies a recognition of guilt and a wish to repair the damage.

Someone persecuted by an excessively harsh superego could be seen as unconsciously cowering under an unstable mountain of guilt. To recognise its scale or to attempt the slightest reduction of its terrible weight is to risk an annihilating avalanche of shame. Such unfortunate people, unable to make any move that would allow the process of reparation to begin, are doomed to endless reproach and attack from within.

People whose superego is this cruel usually have to get rid of it one way or another, otherwise they are in great danger of hurting themselves or others. In extreme cases, relationships are damaged and acute depression causes difficulties at work. At its worst, suicide or even murder can seem to be the only way to silence the remorseless internal assault.

The superego located outside in someone else

Sometimes when the superego is too fierce – when guilt feels too awful to bear – people *project* their superego outside themselves into someone else. What this means is that they locate the criticising voices in somebody else and experience the criticism as coming from that other person. The person who they feel is criticising them may not be criticising them at all. A peculiar look, or a chance remark, or a missed opportunity to telephone, can all seem like signs of someone being critical and censorious. Thinking someone else is persecuting you or finding fault with you can be a terrible experience, but nothing like as painful as hating yourself, a situation from which there can be no respite. Sometimes people can become quite paranoid as a defence against their own unconscious guilt.

Here is an example: Helene Deutsch writes about a patient of hers who was unable to pay her analytic fees for some time. The patient, instead of being grateful for the analyst's patience, became extremely aggressive. She began searching through the past couple of years of analysis, 'remembering' slights from the analyst, ways the analyst had misunderstood her or mistreated her. Dr. Deutsch describes these as,

a flood of recollections of minor incidents that had occurred during the analysis and which she was able to twist to suit her purposes. [. . .] She maintained, for instance, that her analysis, and her whole future, had already been ruined by a telephone conversation which had curtailed her session by a few minutes [and she insisted that] *I had done this because of my deep antipathy for her. By casting the blame on me she was able to keep herself free from guilt and therefore also free from depression.*[9]

This example demonstrates a way in which people can fend off feelings of guilt by blaming others for persecuting or criticising them. Thus somebody else is identified as the persecutor, and that somebody is the one who ought to feel guilty.

To escape from unconscious and unbearable guilt, some people will attempt to provoke censoriousness from others. Freud wrote about people he described as 'criminals from a sense of guilt', who are threatened with feelings of badness they can neither understand nor bear, people whose guilty feelings are so powerful that they are only relieved when they actually do something that is bad.[10] There are two reasons for this. In the first place, actually doing something bad makes the guilt feelings seem rational; the crime, however bad it is, is limited and located in the real world and therefore 'dealable with'. Second, the punishment that follows the actual misdeed can temporarily alleviate some of the guilt feelings. This is because punishment from outside authorities may be less devastating than the punishment meted out by a very severe superego.

The superego inside yourself but directed at someone outside

This is a common way of dealing with a harsh superego – instead of allowing it to persecute himself, the person turns it towards other people in his life and persecutes them. James Thurber wrote a story about a man whose son was afraid of other children. The man urges his son to stand up to the bullies; he insists that the boy has to fight them. The little boy tries to do what his father wants, but as he confronts the bullies he gets too afraid and runs away. The father's reaction is to shout at his son, to bully the boy every bit as badly as the other children did: 'You snivelling creep! You good-for-nothing little coward!'

We can understand this story as being about the father's unsuccessful fight with his own bullying superego. We can guess that the man has had some experience of being denigrated and belittled in his own mind by a very cruel and bullying part of himself that tells him he's a coward and no good and useless and a pathetic baby. This voice may have come from his own actual father, but it is now inside him, always threatening him with harsh criticism and contempt. So what does he do about this awful situation? He gets rid of this voice directed at himself and turns it on his son; the son becomes an object of his contempt and he himself is free from criticism.

We all know people like this – people who strike us as bossy or forbidding or 'head-mistressy'. They manage to make us feel small, or clumsy or stupid. Next time you run into one, it may help to remember that they are more than likely getting rid of their own bad feelings by putting them into you.

The psychoanalytic concept of the superego

How does our superego get established inside each of us? How do we become moral or civilised? How is it that we obey the law, treat each other fairly, respect each other's rights? We stop at red traffic lights in the middle of the night, when no one would know if we didn't; we leave other people's property alone, though we wouldn't be caught if we snatched it; we consider it fair that the less fortunate in society should be looked after and protected by the more fortunate. Not entirely, of course, but mostly. Each of us contains our own guiding and prohibiting moral policeman. But how does it happen? How does the entirely selfish baby turn into the civilised adult? How do we get a superego?

The simple answer that Freud gave is that we owe our conscience to our experience of the authoritative, judgemental, critical and punitive aspects of our parents, particularly, he thought, of our father. Judgements (in fact, whole ways of thinking about right and wrong) accepted from our parents when we were too young to question them are, during childhood, taken inside us and set up as an authority inside ourselves – as our own superego.

In this way our parents, and their views and qualities, and later the views and qualities of other people we are close to or admire, become parts of ourselves. Our personalities are very much affected by the important people with whom we've identified in our lives, particularly our early lives. And our superego is the primary example of how identifications can profoundly affect our personalities: someone with a very strict, harsh superego is immediately recognisable as different from someone with a laid-back, more forgiving attitude towards himself. This is not a value judgement: one personality is not necessarily better than the other, each can have strengths and each weaknesses; but they are different personalities.

In the following section I describe the theoretical underpinning to the psychoanalytic concept of the superego. This will necessarily involve using concepts and ideas that are complex and sometimes difficult to grasp.

Introjection and identification: how the superego is formed

Psychoanalytic understanding of the way we each come to have a superego developed over many years, but it began with the attempts of Freud and another early psychoanalyst, Karl Abraham, to understand and treat patients who were suffering from what was then called *melancholia* (a condition we would now call *depression*). What they noticed was that patients suffering from 'melancholia' criticise themselves constantly – they accuse themselves of worthlessness, of badness, of unkindness, of not caring about anybody but themselves, about not really being able to do anything well at all, about letting their loved ones (parents, friends, spouses) down, and so on. This self-criticism, sometimes amounting to self-hatred, is the primary distinguishing characteristic of depression. Abraham noticed that people who are very depressed seem very much like people in mourning, but that it was not clear who or what exactly had been lost or had died. Furthermore, it seemed to be a kind of mourning gone haywire: extended and excessive as well as seemingly unwarranted.[11] This theory – that depression equals mourning gone haywire – has remained the basic psycho-analytic theory of depression. Its elaboration during the years that followed led to an under-standing not only of depression as an illness, but also of the concept of a superego existing inside each individual, and of the relationship between superego functions and depressive illnesses.

Abraham exploited the comparison between grief at mourning and depression to explain the reason for the latter; he said that while both mourning and depression represent the response to a loss, in depression there is an unconscious *hostility* at play. In other words, the distinction between depression and normal mourning processes is that in depression there is a great deal of anger present. He went on to suggest that an individual is likely to pass over the bounds of normal mourning into abnormal depression when his reaction to the loss of someone he loves is heavily charged with anger and even hate. This was a brilliant insight, based on sharp clinical observation: a depressed person is not just miserable, he's furious.

In 1916 Freud continued and greatly extended the study of depression in a major theoretical paper that established the model for an understanding of the processes of 'introjection' and 'identification', and thus paved the way for an understanding of the establishment of the superego. In this paper, 'Mourning and Melancholia', Freud accepts Abraham's theory intact. He, too, stresses the relationship between mourning and depression, and sees both of them as a reaction to the loss – through death, disappointment or betrayal – of a loved object (that is to say, a person, thing or institution that has been the object of powerful feelings).[12] And he agrees with Abraham about the presence of hostility in the depressed person. But Freud goes on to make another important distinction: he says that while mourning is always in relation to a consciously perceived, actually lost object; melancholia, while it may be in relation to a similar object, is more frequently experienced in relation to a loss that can only be located in the Unconscious.

Freud spelt out the characteristics shared by people who are mourning someone who has died or gone away, with people who are obviously deeply depressed but where there is no obvious evidence of loss. These shared characteristics are familiar to all of us, and include a painful dejection, a withdrawal of interest in the outside world, inhibition of activity and a loss of the capacity to feel loving towards available figures. But in addition, says Freud, depressives show certain features that normal mourners don't usually suffer from: a terrible loss of self-esteem, self-accusation and even a delusional need for punishment. He elaborated a theoretical system to explain all of these clinical features. (These feelings are, of course, experienced at moments by many people going through ordinary mourning; but when they become intractable and last for an extended period, psychoanalysts and others feel that the mourning process has become complicated by depression.)

What Freud said was that in both ordinary mourning and depression, there is a loss – either in reality or phantasy – of a loved object. In normal mourning there follows an extremely slow and painful process in which all of the interest and energy which had until that point been directed at this object are slowly and painfully withdrawn from it in a process of separation. This is always extremely painful, as anyone who has lost someone dear to them can attest. But in normal mourning this painful unhappy process proceeds along a progressive course: very gradually, interest, thoughts, feelings are withdrawn from the lost person; there is a step-by-step, bit-by-bit detachment, which, in the end, leaves the mourner free to continue with his life: to love someone else, to have other interests.

In depression something else takes place. For someone to fall ill with depression at the loss of a loved one, the relationship with that loved one must have been basically *narcissistic* – that is, the loved object was really felt to *belong to*, to have been a part of or an extension of, the person's own self. So the feeling of impoverishment is experienced in the very self: 'I (without my loved one) am nothing, nothing holds me together, there is nothing of any value in me.' As for the normal mourner, the world is without interest; but for the depressed person the *self* is without capacities to experience interest as well. Samuel Taylor Coleridge describes this experience beautifully in his poem 'Dejection: An Ode'.

And still I gaze – and with how blank an eye!
And those thin clouds above, in flakes and bars,
That give away their motion to the stars;
Those stars, that glide behind them or between,
Now sparkling, now bedimmed, but
      always seen:
Yon crescent Moon, as fixed as if it grew
In its own cloudless, starless lake of blue;
I see them all so excellently fair,
I see, not feel, how beautiful they are!

My genial spirits fail;
And what can these avail
To lift the smothering weight from off my breast?

It were a vain endeavour,
Though I should gaze forever
On that green light that lingers in the west:
I may not hope from outward forms to win
The passion and the life, whose fountains
          are within.[13]

Furthermore, in depression not only is one's self experienced as incapable of feeling interested in the world, and unable to be loving towards anyone, as Coleridge describes, but also in fact, one's very self becomes the object of enormous hatred, criticism and denigration. People in such a state feel utterly worthless, but, paradoxically, there is also a peculiar aura of self-importance, of self-aggrandisement in their complaints about themselves: 'I am the most useless person in the world'; 'Obviously no one is kind to me; who would want to be the friend of someone so revolting?'; 'Of course I've never been able to hold down a job; I'm just completely lazy and self-destructive I guess', and so on. What Freud noticed about all these complaints that the depressed person makes about himself is that they actually seem to apply, or be directed, much more closely to the person he has lost than they do to him! It began to look as though these harsh criticisms are in fact directed towards the lost object or, at least, towards a part of the self now identified with that object. 'The shadow of the object fell upon the ego,' said Freud, to describe what seems to happen.[14]

This may all appear complicated and hard to understand. It will help to remember that one difference between ordinary mourners and depressed people is that depressives are more angry with their lost loved ones. But this is no ordinary kind of anger, left over from some everyday domestic resentment or disappointment. If someone believes quite literally that the person they love actually belongs to them and therefore has no independent life of his or her own, then the death of that person can seem to be a terrible act of treachery – a betrayal of everything that made the relationship valuable. All is lost, including the past. Awkward and unwelcome anger is denied because it is impossible to acknowledge it, let alone express it, at a time when mourning and sorrow are the only acceptable emotions. Instead, the lost object is *introjected*, taken into the self and identified with, and made a part of, the self.[15] It is then berated, attacked and criticised (for leaving, for dying, for disappointing) by another unidentified-with-the-object part of the self. Thus a part of the self is attacked as if it were the object. What looks as though one part of the self is attacking another part of the self as if a bitter emotional civil war had broken out is, in fact, something quite different. Actually, there *is* a war, but it cannot be acknowledged because it is between the self and an ambivalently loved object. To admit the war would entail letting go of the loved object – giving it, as it were, its freedom. The sense of loss this would involve is unbearable:

In this way an object loss was transformed into an ego loss, and the conflict between the ego and the loved person into a cleavage between the critical activity of the ego, and the ego as altered by identification.[16]

And what is the purpose of this? The purpose is to negate real feelings of loss of the other: in this way, the object is not lost, not mourned and not given up – it is in fact installed within the self and there it remains, to be tortured, punished and controlled.

An example will help here. In his first year of analysis, a patient of mine approached the long summer holiday with complete equanimity. He was glad of the chance not to have to make the car journey for six weeks, to have more time for himself and his family. He certainly did not mind that I was going away. At the end of the summer break he returned to his first session in a terrible state and full of anxiety: he was sure he was going to lose his professional position because he himself had taken a longer summer break from his office than was usual. At the time he arranged this break he had felt completely confident about it, but while he was on holiday it had occurred to him that it was irresponsible, indeed delinquent, to be away from the office for so long, and that it was very likely that everything would have gone wrong in his absence. 'How could I have been so stupid as to plan such a long break?' he asked. It's what he always does, he said: behaves responsibly for a while, then wrecks it with some unconsidered behaviour! Obviously the other partners at the firm would be furious with him because some major business decisions would have had to be taken while he was away and he would not have been around to participate. And again: how could he have been so stupid as to go away for so long? He was going into the office for the first time that morning just after his session and he had no idea how he would face everyone.

It will be clear that this patient was full of what looked like self-persecuting feelings. Some very critical part of him was berating and punishing another part of him for being, among other things, stupid, irresponsible, self-indulgent (taking a longer holiday). But what became clear in the session, as the situation was discussed and more facts came out (that, for instance, he had only taken two days longer than usual, that he had discussed it with several people at work before he'd gone), was that the criticism that was going on in such a torturing way inside his head was much more appropriately directed towards his analyst. *Somebody* had been irresponsible and delinquent. *Somebody* ought to be fired. *Somebody* had left people in the lurch, without the help they needed over the long summer break. *Somebody* was self-indulgently enjoying him- or herself, while other people had to manage without help.

The patient, as we came to see, had 'cured' himself of any threatening feelings of loss or dependency over the holiday. Consciously, he didn't mind that I was going away and he felt very warm towards me. That is, consciously he didn't experience any loss. And in order to protect both of us from his rage at me, he didn't experience the rage with me; instead, a part of him became identified with a felt-to-be irresponsible, delinquent, self-serving me. And he punished that identified-with-me part of himself with remorseless cruelty.

What I hope this example shows is how a conflict that really belongs to a relationship becomes internalised – instead of being between him and me, it is experienced as being between him (who is criticising) and him (who is criticised). In formulating this theory about how external figures become internalised and identified with, Freud was establishing a model for the internalisation of parental figures that become the superego. The theory was: in certain people, a loss is not experienced as a loss; it is experienced as a change in the self. Aspects of the lost object are internalised and identified with: 'I have not lost you; I have become you.'

Here is another example; this one is important because it shows some of this process taking place in a young child. A young family was travelling on a train – parents and two small boys, aged four and two. The mother had brought crayons and paper for the children to play with, but the journey was quite long and both boys began to get tired and fed up with being confined. The older boy, Thomas, began first to walk and then to run up and down the aisles; after a few minutes of this his father, slightly annoyed, grabbed his son and, holding him at his upper arms, said, 'This is not a playground, Thomas.' Thomas looked suitably subdued and sat back down. A few minutes later the younger boy, James, suddenly pulled himself up and stood on the seat, looking out the window, and then climbed up onto the table between the banks of seats. 'This is not a playground James! This is not a playground!' shouted Thomas, himself now the voice of harsh authority.

This seems a common enough story and not very complicated, and we might wonder if it couldn't simply be described as the boy having learnt about acceptable behaviour from his father. But if we go a little bit further in our thinking, we might be able to see that Thomas is not simply telling James what their father said. Thomas has, in a tiny way, *become* his father. He isn't saying (even if he were old enough to speak in this more complicated way) 'Dad says this is not a playground'. He is, in a way, *being* dad, shouting at the naughty child. This is an 'identification' – in this case an identification with a particular authoritarian aspect of his father. Another way psycho-analysts would describe it is as an 'intro-jection'. The boy has taken his father into himself and a part of himself has become identified with his father.

Of course, Thomas is only four years old, and we assume (and hope) that he will keep running up and down the aisles, and doing things his father will tell him not to do, for a few years yet. But gradually his father, telling him what is and isn't allowed, will be more and more *introjected*, and eventually the voice saying 'This is not a playground' will be directed from inside himself at the part of him who has the impulse to misbehave. His super-ego will have become established.

That, as I said earlier, is the simple answer. The child introjects the voice of his parents, which becomes his *internal* authority, his superego. But, of course, the process is *much* more complicated than that because the child's picture of his parents and of their commands and prohibitions, is deeply affected by the child's own feelings. A jealous, angry child often views his parents as being similarly angry and fierce; because he feels horrible inside himself, he sees the whole world, and especially his parents, also as being horrible. He *projects* his bad feelings onto his parents; he imagines them feeling as horrible about him as he does about them. So the father and/ or mother whom he *introjects* are introjected as he imagines them to be – and often this is angrier, harsher, stricter than they actually are. To go back to the last example, Thomas' father may have been a bit cross with Thomas when he stopped him running up and down the aisle of the train. But when Thomas shouted at his brother James, he was much more than cross; he was furious, contemptuous and frightening. He treated James with much more contempt, much more fury than that with which his father spoke to him. This is a familiar picture: little girls spanking their dolls with much more force than ever they were spanked; little boys whose parents have nearly always spoken courteously to them, turning on their small brothers with disdain. This is a reflection of the complicated processes of projection and introjection that go on throughout childhood, from the very beginning of life. A child attributes his feelings, loving and hating, to the important people in his life. When he feels good inside and loving towards his parents, all other things being equal he will imagine them as loving towards him. Picturing them as loving external figures in the real world, he will also have an inside-himself picture of them as loving, and he will identify with this picture of loving parents; this will strengthen his picture of himself as loving. And it works the other way round, too: when he feels full of hate and jealousy and resentment, he imagines his parents as hating him. Although we cannot know what processes were going on inside Thomas, we can make a guess that he felt both betrayed by and angry with his beloved father for being cross with him; his picture of his father was then coloured by his own angry feelings, and it was this now very angry father with whom Thomas identified, and who Thomas was 'being' when he shouted at James.

The superego: heir to the Oedipus complex

In fact, Freud thought that the superego becomes established at just about Thomas's age – between three and five years old, and he linked its establishment to the rich and complex emotional relationships that exist within families, and to the central event in a child's emotional development, the Oedipus complex. To understand the Oedipus complex, and how its resolution leads to the establishment of the superego, we need to understand something about Freud's theory of childhood sexuality.

In 'The Three Essays on The Theory of Sexuality'(first published in 1905, but revised in successive editions) Freud confronted his readers with what was at that time a shocking idea; the notion that human sexuality does not begin suddenly at puberty, but has its beginnings in the very first relationships, physical and emotional, of infantile life. In so doing, Freud deepened and broadened our view of sexuality, by including a baby and young child's very early bodily sensations and earliest love relationships in his wide view of sexuality. He knew his ideas would be disturbing to readers, and they were. Freud noticed, for instance, that when a baby sucks at his mother's breast, the baby sucks not just for nourishment but for pleasure, pleasure that is connected with his mouth. His mouth, which sucks and bites and grasps his mother's nipple, is an organ of pleasure -- Freud described it as his first 'erotogenic zone'. And while he is sucking and licking and later nibbling and biting, he is in a relationship with his mother who is having her own responses to his activities. Pleasure and pain and excitement and fulfilment: it is not hard to see why Freud thought such activities were fundamentally sexual - although not, of course, genital or sexual in a grown-up way.

And it is not at all hard to see why people find this idea disturbing, even repugnant – that a baby sucking at a breast is experiencing a kind of pleasure that can be described in a very general way as 'sexual' – that is, related to particular, changing, excitable areas of his body. But if we understand that it is sexual only in an infantile way, we may perhaps find it easier to allow that it contains the earliest seeds of what will one day be adult sexuality.

Now, during this early 'oral stage' of development, the baby's mouth is particularly sensitive and excitable, and he quite quickly begins to associate the pleasure he gets from sucking with the mother who suckles him. Later, Freud thought, at around the time of toilet training, the small child's special sensitivity moves to his rectum and anus and bladder and urethra, and many of his highly charged exchanges with his mother will revolve around whether he urinates and defecates, and where, and when, and what they both feel about it all.

But at a certain stage in a child's life – Freud thought at around three or four – the child begins to have sensations in his or her genitals – this is the age at which both boys and girls begin to touch and explore their genitals, often to their parents' embarrassment and chagrin. And because the child's mother and father are the objects of his most intense emotional feelings, they, the parents, become the objects of the toddler's sexual desires as well.

Example: a five-year-old boy climbed into bed beside his mother, lined up their two heads so they were perfectly even, and then, motioning down towards an unspecified area under the blankets, somewhere below his chest, said to her, 'Let's just pretend there's a whole lot more of me down there.' Of course this little boy *consciously* meant his height; he could line up his head with his mother's – as he'd often seen his father's head lined up next to his mother's head in the bed – but unlike his father's feet, *his* feet stopped somewhere just below her waist. But his wriggling excitement indicated that he also, unconsciously, meant something else: that he was pretending there was a lot more to him – that he had large powerful genitals like his dad, which would mean he could proudly take his dad's place next to his mum in the big bed.

. . . Thus the Oedipal crisis. The little boy (and it works very similarly for the little girl, the other way round) wants to take his father's place with his mother. On the other hand, he also loves his father and doesn't really want to get rid of him. He's proud that his dad is big and strong, and feels bad, as well as triumphant, when he begins to be able to do things better than his father can. And, at the same time, he is afraid of what his father would do to him if he really tried to take his place . . .

This same little boy sometimes repeated rude words that he had heard his father say. 'You bastard', he would shout at another child, or even at a nasty adult; he obviously thought it was masculine and grown-up and powerful to be able to use rude words. His father, however, did not like his little boy using such words, and quite sternly forbade him to use them. 'But you do it,' the little boy complained. 'And you can too, if you choose to, when you're older,' his father told him. 'Grown-ups are allowed to do some things that children aren't allowed to do.'

What we can see in this example is that there is quite a lot of feeling between these three people: this ordinary mother and father and their ordinary little boy. And among these feelings are love and admiration and desire, and jealousy and rivalry. Freud recognised this configuration of feelings as being not only normal, but also ubiquitous. He named it the

'Oedipus complex' after Sophocles' hero who killed his father and married his mother and then, when he realised what he'd done, put out his own eyes.

The Oedipus complex refers to the crisis that occurs in the life of every young child when he begins to realise that he cannot, and will never be able to, completely possess the parent of the opposite sex: when little boys have to face the fact that they cannot marry their mothers, and little girls have to face the fact that they will never marry their fathers. The boy's wish to possess his mother, for instance, places him in conflict with his father; he wants to take his mother away from his father and he is afraid that his father will be angry with and punish him – even castrate him – for his rivalrous wishes. He links his father's obvious disapproval of his sexual excitement with his own secret feelings of jealousy and competitiveness towards his father.

Of course in describing this complex we have to use words that no child who is the protagonist of such a struggle could ever use about himself. No small child could describe his Oedipus complex in words; yet Oedipal struggles create powerful, deeply charged feelings in every child, feelings so deeply charged that they have to be repressed. In order to repress them, the child renounces the desired parent as the object of all his love, but in order to do this he has to do something else as well. The conflict-creating Oedipal impulses are finally dealt with by a massive internalisation of parental constraints and prohibitions. These internalised constraints prevent even the contemplation of the Oedipal impulses: they are permanently repressed. And thus the superego – for that is what these internalised restraints and prohibitions evolve into – becomes 'the heir to the Oedipus complex'. The child, from this period on, will carry within him his own critical voice, his own censoring agency, his own superego. The particular qualities of any individual child's relationship with his super-ego will depend on how he has managed the intense and complex emotional connections with his parents throughout his infancy and childhood, and particularly how he manages the critical events of the Oedipal period.

Recent psychoanalytic developments

While all psychoanalysts agree about the central importance of the Oedipus complex in psychological development, and about the significant part it plays in the formation of the superego, some psychoanalysts date the beginnings of both much earlier than Freud did. In particular, Melanie Klein, whose work developed from and extended Freud's studies, found evidence of early forms of the superego and of the Oedipus complex in the small children she analysed, and she eventually came to feel that a primitive superego and primitive 'Oedipal' experiences exist from very early on in a baby's life. Her work led her to the conclusion that babies, from a young age, have powerful feelings, and often feel very anxious about the angry, aggressive phantasies that they inevitably have at times about their parents. A baby who feels furious about being left on his own while his parents talk or laugh or cuddle each other may imagine that his violent screams are actually doing violence to his parents; after all, his screams are the only weapon he has. He may then feel anxious that he has *actually* attacked his parents, and imagine them as damaged and even vengefully attacking him back. Later, as his sense of himself and his love for his parents grows stronger, he will feel the beginnings of guilt and sadness about the angry attacks he will inevitably sometimes subject them to. These feelings of persecutory anxiety, and later guilt, were understood by Klein as the beginnings of the child's superego. She felt that as soon as the baby begins to realise that the mother and father he loves are also the mother and father he sometimes hates – because they frustrate him, because they are together without him, because they go away from him – he will begin to feel sad and guilty about the attacks he makes on them. She described this state of mind in the baby – and later in the adult – as the 'depressive position', and for her it is related to the working through of the Oedipus complex and the establishment of a healthy and helpful superego.

Conclusion

Having a superego is an inevitable and necessary part of the human experience; we all live with an internal judge. Our superego can be cruel and persecuting, or it can be relatively benign and forgiving. We can experience it within ourselves or we can project it onto other people, or we can turn it on others and judge them harshly instead of ourselves. Each individual's relationship to his superego develops out of his relationships – in phantasy and in reality – with his parents and other significant figures in his life, and is a reflection of these. And each person's relationship to his superego will also have an effect on his new relationships with other people in his life, as well as his feelings about, and image of, himself.

Notes

1. Freud, S., *The Ego and the Id* (1923), in *Standard Edition of the Complete Psychological Works of Sigmund Freud* (hereafter *SE*), Vol. 19, trans. James Strachey, London: Hogarth Press, 1953–73, pp. 1–66.

2. Freud, S., 'Civilisation and its Discontents' (1930), in *SE*, Vol. 21, pp. 61, 71.

3. Freud, S., 'Humour' (1927), in *SE*, Vol. 21. Also see Freud, S., 'Analysis of a Phobia in a Five-Year-Old Boy', in *SE*, Vol. 10.

4. Klein believes that unconscious phantasies accompany, shape and organise all our behaviour. The word 'phantasy' with a 'ph', is differentiated from 'fantasy', which denotes a conscious daydream. According to Kleinian theory, 'phantasies are the life of the unconscious mind. They are primitive and in some cases permanent phantasies which the ego has about itself and its relation to its internal objects, and they become the basis of the structure of the personality.' (Riesenberg-Malcolm, R., *On Bearing Unbearable States of Mind*, introduction by P. Roth (ed.), London: Routledge, 1999, pp. 2–3.) See Klein, M., *The Psychoanalysis of Children* (1932), London: Karnac Books, 1998; *Contributions to Psychoanalysis* 1921–1945, London: Hogarth Press, 1965.

5. Kaplan, F., *Dickens*, John Curtis (ed.), London: Hodder and Stoughton, 1988, p. 534.

6. Yates, E., from a letter quoted in Kaplan, F., op. cit., p. 534.

7. Kaplan, F., op. cit., p. 538

8. Ibid., p. 538.

9. Deutsch, H., *Neuroses and Character Types, Clinical Psychoanalytic Studies*, New York: International Universities Press, 1965, p. 205.

10. Freud, S., 'Some character types met with in psychoanalytic work, Part III: Criminals from a sense of guilt', in *SE*, Vol. 14, pp. 332–333.

11. Abraham, K., 'Notes on the psychoanalytic investigation and treatment of manic-depressive insanity' (1912), in *Selected Papers of Karl Abraham*, London: Karnac Books, 1988. Also, Freud, S., 'Mourning and Melancholia' (1917), in *SE*, Vol. 14, pp. 237–258.

12. An 'object' is someone or something about whom one has powerful feelings. An 'object' is often a person: one's mother, or husband or best friend are all one's 'objects' in the sense that one's feelings about them often dictate how one feels about oneself. Sometimes an institution (England, say, or Manchester United Football Club) can be one of someone's objects; so, for instance, I might feel terrible if my team lost an important match. And sometimes an idea can become like an object, so that anyone who attacks it is felt to be a dangerous enemy. The term 'loss of the object' can refer to the death of the loved person, but it can equally refer

to a sense that one has lost one's feelings of love for the object; that the object has lost its particular position in one's mind.

13. Coleridge, S.T., 'Dejection: An Ode', in Frank Kermode and John Hollander (eds), *The Oxford Anthology of English Literature*, New York: Oxford University Press, Vol. II, 1973, pp. 276–277.

14. Freud, S., 1917, op. cit., p. 249.

15. Many of Freud's later theories come directly from this idea of a process of internalisation ('identification', or 'introjection'). In 1921 he used the idea of 'identification' as a basis for a revision of his theory of social groups. The solidarity in groups, the 'glue' that sticks people together, is an identification they have in common. They all introject the same person (or idea) as a central part of themselves (their egos). Christians, for instance, are joined in their central belief in Christ, and they each 'carry' him in their heart (see R.D. Hinshelwood, *Clinical Klein*, London: Free Association Books, 1994, p. 20).

16. Freud, S., 1917, op. cit., p. 249.

Dedication

For Nick